88 Special Greek Salad Recipes

(88 Special Greek Salad Recipes - Volume 1)

Terra Mincy

Content

88 Awesome Greek Salad Recipes

***

1. Bacon Feta Greek Pasta Salad Recipe

Serving: 6 | Prep: | Cook: 20mins | Ready in:

Ingredients

- 1 (12 oz) package of whole wheat penne pasta
- 3 slices turkey bacon, cooked and crumbled
- 1 green bell pepper, chopped
- 1 red bell pepper, chopped
- 1 cup baby spinach, chopped
- 1/2 cucumber, chopped
- 1/4 cup black olives, sliced
- 8 pepperoncini peppers, chopped
- 1 tomato, chopped
- 1 red onion, sliced
- 1/2 cup Absolutely Fabulous Greek/House Dressing (from this AllRecipes)
- 1/2 cup feta, crumbled

Direction

- Bring a large saucepan full of water to a boil. Once boiling, add the pasta and let it cook for about 8 minutes or until it is al dente.
- Meanwhile, in a skillet sprayed with cooking spray, add the bacon and cook per package directions.
- Once the pasta is done, drain it well.
- Add the drained pasta to a large bowl. Add the bacon, red and green bell pepper and vegetables. Pour the dressing on top and toss until thoroughly distributed. Top with crumbled feta cheese.

2. Chick Peas And Parsley Salad Recipe

Serving: 0 | Prep: | Cook: 12mins | Ready in:

Ingredients

- 400g tin chickpeas , drained and rinsed
- red onion , cut into thin wedges
- ¼ cucumber , halved lengthways and sliced diagonally
- a small bunch flat-leaf parsley , roughly chopped
- 100g feta cheese , crumbled
- 2-3 tbsp extra virgin olive oil
- a small handful basil leaves , roughly chopped
- salt and 1/4 lemon squeezed

Direction

- Put the chickpeas, onion, cucumber, parsley, feta and basil in a large bowl and toss well to combine. Mix the red wine vinegar and 3 tbsp. extra-virgin olive oil together and season well. Pour over the salad and toss.

3. Chicken Caesar Salad Recipe Recipe

Serving: 4 | Prep: | Cook: | Ready in:

Ingredients

- 2 romaine lettuce,torn into pieces
- 200g cherry tomatoes
- 600g chicken breast fillets
- 200g streaky bacon
- 2 cups croutons, garlic flavoured
- 100g Parmesan shavings
- 100ml olive oil
- salt and black pepper to taste

- Caesar Dressing
- 1 egg yolk
- 1 clove garlic, crushed
- 2 tbs lemon juice
- 1 tsp Dijon mustard
- 3 anchovy fillets, canned and drained
- 100ml olive oil
- salt and black pepper to taste

Direction

- Brush chicken fillets with olive oil, season with salt and pepper and grill until cooked through, about 10-15 minutes.
- Cut bacon into small pieces and fry in oil until crispy.
- Slice chicken thinly and place in a large salad bowl with bacon, lettuce, tomatoes and garlic croutons.
- Toss with Caesar dressing and serve with a garnish of parmesan shavings.
- To prepare Caesar dressing place egg yolk, garlic, lemon juice, mustard and anchovies in a blender and mix until smooth.
- Gradually add oil and continue blending until dressing thickens.
- Season with salt and pepper to taste.

4. Chopped Greek Salad With Chicken Recipe

Serving: 4 | Prep: | Cook: | Ready in:

Ingredients

- 1/3 cup red-wine vinegar
- 2 tablespoons extra virgin olive oil
- 1 tablespoon chopped fresh dill or oregano or 1 teaspoon dried
- 1-teaspoon garlic powder
- ¼-teaspoon salt
- ¼ teaspoon freshly ground pepper
- 6 cups chopped cos (romaine) lettuce
- Two ½ cups chopped cooked chicken (about 12 ounces; see Tip)
- 2 medium tomatoes, chopped
- 1 medium cucumber, peeled, seeded and chopped
- ½ cup finely chopped red onion
- ½ cup sliced ripe black olives
- ½ cup crumbled feta cheese

Direction

- Whisk the vinegar, oil, dill, (or oregano), garlic powder, salt and pepper in a large bowl. Add lettuce, chicken, tomatoes, cucumber, onion, olives and feta; toss to coat if you don't have cooked chicken, poach 1-pound chicken breasts for this recipe. Place boneless, skinless chicken breasts in a medium skillet or saucepan. Add lightly salted water (or chicken stock) to cover and bring to a boil. Cover, reduce heat to low and simmer gently until the chicken is cooked through and no longer pink in the middle, 10 to 15 minutes.

5. Chopped Greek Salad With Garlic Croutons Recipe

Serving: 8 | Prep: | Cook: 12mins | Ready in:

Ingredients

- garlic CROUTONS:
- 3 c bread crumbs, 3/4 inch cubes are good. (Cut from day old, sturdy bread with crusts remeoved)
- 1/3 c EVOO
- 2 large garlic cloves, thinly sliced
- 2 T flat leaf parlsey, finely chopped
- 1 t finely grated lemon zest
- kosher salt
- fresh ground black pepper
- DRESSING:
- 1/2 c fragrant evoo
- 1/4 c red or white wine vinegar, or fresh lemon juice
- 2 T finely chopped shallots
- 1 t Dijon mustard

- 1 t chopped fresh oregano
- 1 t mashed oil-packed anchoves (2-4 filets)
- kosher salt
- fresh ground black pepper
- SALAD:
- 4 c gently packe baby arugula, washed and dried
- 3 medium firm-ripe tomatoes, cored, seeded and diced (about 2 c)
- 1 med english cucumber, seeded and diced (about 2 cups)
- 1 c meaty Kalamata or Cerignola olives, pitted and quartered
- 1/2 lb firm feta cheese, cut into 1/2 inch dice, (about 1 1/2 c)

Direction

- GARLIC CROUTONS:
- Preheat oven to 375, with rack in center
- Put bread cubes in large bowl
- In small saucepan, heat oil and garlic, over med heat, until garlic begins to color, 3-5 min being careful not to burn
- Pour the oil through a strainer onto bread crumbs
- Toss until evenly coated
- Transfer to baking sheet and toast the bread in oven, flipping occasionally, until golden on all sides, and still somewhat soft in middle, about 12 minutes
- Return to bowl while still warm and toss with remaining crouton ingredients
- DRESSING
- In a medium bowl, whisk the EVOO and vinegar or lemon juice, shallots, mustard, oregano and anchovies. Add salt and pepper to taste.
- Let sit for at least 10 minutes
- SALAD:
- Lay the arugula on a large platter and artfully arrange veggies, cheese, and croutons in stripes or piles
- Whisk the dressing again and pour into a small pitcher to serve, or, drizzle over entire salad just before serving (may not need all of the dressing).

6. Couscous Salad Recipe

Serving: 6 | Prep: | Cook: 10mins | Ready in:

Ingredients

- For the dressing
- 2 T . Olive oil
- 2 T . Fresh lemon juice
- 1/4 t.. Salt
- Ground black pepper to taste
- For the salad
- 1 1/2 cups of water , or chicken broth
- 1 t. olive oil
- 1 cup couscous
- 1 cup quartered cherry or grape tomatoes
- 5 T. pitted , sliced Kalamata olives
- 5 T. fresh parsley , chopped
- 4 o.z. feta cheese , crumbled

Direction

- Whisk dressing ingredients in a small bowl, and set aside.
- In medium sauce pan, heat water, (or chicken broth), and olive oil to a boil.
- Stir in couscous, cover and remove from heat.
- Let stand 3 mins. Uncover, and fluff with a fork.
- Place couscous in a medium serving bowl.
- Pour dressing ingredients over couscous, and toss with a fork.
- Add tomatoes, olives, parsley, and feta cheese. Toss to combine.
- Serve hot, or at room temp.

7. Creamy Coleslaw

Serving: 6 | Prep: | Cook: 10mins | Ready in:

Ingredients

- 1 package (14 ounces) coleslaw mix
- 3/4 cup mayonnaise
- 1/3 cup sour cream
- 1/4 cup sugar
- 3/4 teaspoon seasoned salt
- 1/2 teaspoon ground mustard
- 1/4 teaspoon celery salt

Direction

- Place coleslaw mix in a large bowl. In a small bowl, combine the remaining ingredients; stir until blended. Pour over coleslaw mix and toss to coat. Refrigerate until serving.
- Test Kitchen Tips
- Greek yogurt can be used instead of sour cream for less fat and more protein.
- If you like your coleslaw tart, add 1/4 cup vinegar or lemon juice or maybe even a julienned Granny Smith apple.
- Nutrition Facts
- 3/4 cup: 283 calories, 24g fat (5g saturated fat), 19mg cholesterol, 431mg sodium, 13g carbohydrate (11g sugars, 2g fiber), 1g protein.

8. Creamy Garden Salad With Tuna Recipe

Serving: 1 | Prep: | Cook: 15mins |Ready in:

Ingredients

- 1/3 cup non-fat plain Greek yogurt
- 1/2 tsp grainy mustard
- 1 clove garlic, minced
- 1 tsp lemon juice
- 1 tsp coarse-ground black pepper
- fresh dill, to taste
- 150g fresh tomatoes, chopped (about 2 "cocktail" sized ones)
- 100g cucumber, diced
- 1 medium slice red onion, diced
- 80g canned chunk tuna (in water), drained and flaked

- 1/2 head iceberg lettuce

Direction

- In a medium bowl, whisk together yogurt, mustard, garlic, lemon juice, pepper and dill.
- Add tomatoes, cucumber, onion and tuna and stir well to mix everything. Let stand 10 minutes for the flavours to blend.
- Shred the lettuce into a large salad bowl, top with the yogurt mixture and enjoy!

9. Cretan Style Bruschetta Salad Kritikos Dakos Recipe

Serving: 4 | Prep: | Cook: |Ready in:

Ingredients

- 3/4 cup Feta cheese; crumbled
- 1 teaspoon oregano
- 2 tablespoons Kalamata olives; chopped
- 1/2 cup ripe tomatoes; chopped
- 3 tablespoons olive oil
- 4 Cretan barley rusks

Direction

- Combine first five ingredients in a bowl and place in refrigerator for at least an hour or overnight.
- Sprinkle rusks with a few drops of water to moisten slightly.
- Top each rusk with the prepared cheese and tomato mixture.
- Set aside for 10 minutes and then serve with a chilled glass of white wine.

10. Cucumber Dill Greek Yogurt Salad Recipe

Serving: 6 | Prep: | Cook: 15mins |Ready in:

Ingredients

- http://shewearsmanyhats.com
- Cucumber Dill Greek Yogurt Salad
- Prep time
- 15 mins
- Total time
- 15 mins
- Author: ©Amy Johnson | She Wears Many Hats
- Serves: 6
- Ingredients
- •4 large cucumbers (about 2 pounds)
- •4 tablespoon plain greek yogurt (I used 0% fat)
- •1 tablespoon dill
- •1 tablespoon rice vinegar (substitute red or white wine vinegar if needed)
- •½ teaspoon sugar
- •½ teaspoon salt
- •¼ teaspoon black pepper
- •¼ teaspoon garlic powder

Direction

- Instructions
- Peel, half, seed, and slice cucumbers.
- In a medium bowl combine yogurt, dill, vinegar, sugar, salt, pepper and garlic powder.
- Add cucumber to bowl and toss with yogurt/dill mixture until combined well.
- Additional salt and pepper to taste, if needed.
- Refrigerate covered until ready to serve.

11. Da Jacks Blue Cheese Dressing Recipe

Serving: 10 | Prep: | Cook: |Ready in:

Ingredients

- 2/3 cup of olive oil
- 1/2 cup of fresh squeezed lime juice with pulp
- 3 to 4 ounces crumbled blue cheese (or Roquefort)

Direction

- Mix ingredients, shake and taste. You may want to adjust the oil / lime juice proportions based on your taste.

12. Dill Orzo Pasta Salad With Cucumber And Feta Recipe

Serving: 8 | Prep: | Cook: 10mins |Ready in:

Ingredients

- orzo pasta Salad with Tomato, cucumber, red onions and feta Ingredients
- 1 lb orzo pasta
- 1 sm English cucumber; peeled,
- 1/4 c olive oil
- 1/2 c Coarsely chopped fresh dill (or more, to taste)
- 1 cup champagne vinegar
- 1/2 c rice wine vinegar
- 1 sm Red onion; minced
- 1/2 lb Feta cheese; crumbled (FRENCH FETA is creamier and works best)
- 1 lg clove garlic; minced
- salt and pepper
- 1 pt Yellow cherry tomatoes

Direction

- Instructions for Orzo Pasta Salad with Tomato, Cucumber, Red Onions and Feta
- Boil orzo until just tender, about 8 minutes.
- Drain and transfer to a bowl.
- Add vinegar immediately and let cool a bit.
- Add oil, onion, dill and garlic and stir well.
- When pasta is cooled to room temp, add cherry tomatoes, cucumber, dill and vinegar. Add feta, salt and pepper and stir gently.
- Chill for several hours to allow flavors to meld.

13. Fabulous Greek House Dressing Recipe

Serving: 30 | Prep: | Cook: | Ready in:

Ingredients

- 1 1/2 quarts olive oil
- 1/3 cup garlic powder
- 1/3 cup dried oregano
- 1/3 cup dried basil
- 1/4 cup pepper
- 1/4 cup salt
- 1/4 cup onion powder
- 1/4 cup dijon-style mustard
- 2 quarts red wine vinegar

Direction

- In a very large container, mix together the olive oil, garlic powder, oregano, basil, pepper, salt, onion powder, and Dijon-style mustard.
- Pour in the vinegar, and mix vigorously until well blended.
- Store tightly covered at room temperature.

14. Forest Fruit Salad Recipe

Serving: 2 | Prep: | Cook: | Ready in:

Ingredients

- 200 gr. red forest fruits (red currants, raspberries, blueberries)
- seeds of a pomegranate
- 40 gr. walnuts
- 40 gr. pinenuts
- 1 tangerine in slices
- 1 bunch green salad
- 1 bunch red salad or radichio
- 1/8 tsp pepper
- 2 spring onions chopped
- 100 gr. chicken breast boiled and cut in small pieces
- 1 tbs chives chopped
- For the dressing
- juice of 2 tangerines
- 3 tbs olive oil
- 1 tsp mustard spicy

Direction

- Break the salad leaves by hand and put them in a large deep bowl.
- Top with the chicken pieces.
- Add the pine nuts, the pomegranate seeds and the red fruits.
- Garnish with the tangerine slices, spring onions and walnuts.
- In another bowl mix the olive oil, tangerine juice and mustard until you get a smooth liquid.
- Pour over the salad and sprinkle the chives on top.

15. Fresh Greek Pasta Salad Recipe

Serving: 10 | Prep: | Cook: 35mins | Ready in:

Ingredients

- 1 box whole wheat shell pasta
- 2 boneless, skinless chicken breasts (thawed)
- 1 medium yellow onion, diced
- 1 cup grape tomatoes, quartered
- 2 large cucumbers, peeled & cut into 1-inch chunks
- 10 kalamata olives, minced
- 2 cups feta cheese, crumbled
- 1 can cannellini beans
- 1/2 cup white wine vinegar
- 2/3 cup dry white wine, plus more for deglazing
- 1/4 cup Italian dressing
- 1/8 cup milk
- 1/2 cup olive oil, plus more for browning chicken
- 1 tbsp: oregano, coriander, garlic powder, cumin

- 1 tsp: salt & freshly ground black pepper
- handful fresh flat-leaf parsley, finely chopped

Direction

- Coat the bottom of a Dutch oven with olive oil and heat. Rub chicken with seasonings and brown about 3 minutes on each side. Turn down the heat and deglaze with a splash of white wine. Add onion and cook until translucent. Stir in the white wine vinegar, Italian dressing, milk, and the rest of the white wine, and bring to a simmer. Cover and cook for about 25 minutes, or until chicken is no longer pink inside. Remove chicken to a bowl and let rest at least 5 minutes. Take the Dutch oven off of the burner and let dressing cool uncovered.
- Meanwhile, boil water in a large pot and cook pasta until "al dente". Drain in a colander and rinse with cold water; transfer to a large bowl. Add the tomatoes, cucumbers, olives. Drain and rinse the beans, add to bowl. Drizzle with a bit of olive oil and mix gently.
- Once chicken has rested, shred with two forks, and transfer to the pasta bowl.
- Once dressing has cooled, stir in feta cheese. Mix into the pasta and top with the parsley. Serve cold.

16. Fresh Greek Salad Recipe

Serving: 4 | Prep: | Cook: |Ready in:

Ingredients

- 1 med. red onion, finely diced
- 1-2 c. grape tomatoes
- 1 red pepper, diced
- 1 c. pitted black olives
- ½ c. shredded basil
- ½ lb. crumbled feta
- ½ c.extra virgin olive oil
- pepper

Direction

- If you can't find grape tomatoes use cherry tomatoes cut in two. I use red pepper because of the extra nutrition in red foods. Take a break and buy yourself pitted black olives. If not, use the royal olives with the purple skin. Use the flat edge of a knife to flatten the olive with your fist, which makes for easy pitting. Don't use feta from a tub--buy something fresh from the deli. I prefer cow feta, but goat feta can be nice too. Some delis wrap your feta in brown paper, but put it in a container and keep it covered with water to keep it fresh if you don't use it right away. Extra virgin olive oil is a must - use a good quality one and the flavour will be amazing. Once you blend the ingredients let the salad stand for a few minutes so the flavours mingle. Yummers!

17. Fresh Greek(ish) Salad With Goat Cheese Vinaigrette And Pita Croutons Recipe

Serving: 4 | Prep: | Cook: 20mins |Ready in:

Ingredients

- 5-6 cups mixed greens(I always try to toss in some bitter "greens" too like radicchio or arugula, etc)
- 1 cucumber, sliced thin(I don't peel)
- 8-12 cherry tomatoes, halved
- 1/2 red onion, sliced thin
- 1 bell pepper, chopped
- For Pita Croutons
- 2 6in(or so) round flat breads, cut into bite sized pieces
- 3T olive oil or melted butter
- 1T dry mixed Greek herbs(the blend I use has sage, oregano, thyme, basil, dill)
- 1t lemon zest
- kosher or sea salt and fresh ground black
- For goat cheese Vinaigrette

- 2oz sun dried tomato goat cheese
- juice from 1 lemon
- 1-2t honey
- 3T red wine vinegar
- about 1/4 cup olive oil
- 1T Dijon
- 2 cloves garlic, crushed into paste
- 2t above Greek type seasoning
- about 1/4 cup salad quality olive oil
- kosher or sea salt and fresh ground black pepper

Direction

- For Croutons
- Toss all ingredients together and spread on baking sheet or stone.
- Bake at 400 for about 12 minutes, until browning. Remove and set aside.
- For Vinaigrette
- Combine all ingredients, other than oil, in medium glass bowl.
- Whisk together until well blended.
- Add olive oil and whisk well.
- Serve salad greens topped with cucumbers, tomatoes, pepper, onion, croutons and dressing.

18. Fresh Summer Salad Recipe

Serving: 4 | Prep: | Cook: 10mins | Ready in:

Ingredients

- 1/2 container of baby heirloom tomatoes
- 1 english cucumber
- 1/4-1/2 vidallia onion
- 4 roasted red peppers
- some peperoncinni spicy peppers (as much or little as you like)
- 1/2 sweet yellow pepper
- 4 oz. feta cheese
- salt and pepper
- Trader Joe's Greek feta salad dressing (to taste)
- Fresh oregano sprinkled on top

Direction

- Cut bigger tomatoes in half or quarters, leave tiny ones whole.
- Dice everything else around the same size.
- Add enough dressing to just "wet" everything (you want to taste the sweetness of all the veggies and NOT just dressing)
- I served this salad with garlic and oregano grilled chicken and roasted garlic teeny tiny potatoes.
- I hope you enjoy this salad as much as my husband and I did!!!!

19. GREEK SALAD DRESSING Recipe

Serving: 1 | Prep: | Cook: | Ready in:

Ingredients

- 1/2 cup olive oil
- 1/4 cup lemon juice
- 1 tsp salt
- 1/2 tsp sugar (optional)
- 1/2 tsp dried oregano leaves, crushed
- 1 clove garlic, minced fine

Direction

- Combine all ingredients in cruet and shake well.
- Store in refrigerator up to 2 weeks.
- Let stand at room temperature before serving.
- Makes 1 cup.

20. Garreys' Potato Salad Recipe

Serving: 5 | Prep: | Cook: 30mins | Ready in:

Ingredients

- 10 Russet potatos'

- 1 package any bacon
- 5 dill pickles
- 1 cup mayo
- 3 table spoons of mustard
- 1/2 tsp pepper
- 1/2 tsp salt

Direction

- Chop potatoes in large cubes, bring to boil till tender
- Let cool naturally or cool with cold water, peel
- Fry bacon till crispy, drain
- In large Bowl/glass dish add potatoes & mayo, stir till completely mixed
- Chop pickles into small pieces. Then add pickles to potatoes, mix well
- Chop bacon and add to mixture.
- Add pepper and salt & mustard
- **have to do it separately as you taste each flavor individually**

21. Greek Style Creamy Dressing Recipe

Serving: 4 | Prep: | Cook: 40mins | Ready in:

Ingredients

- 10 garlic cloves, peeled, divided
- 2/3 cup water
- 5 oz low-fat silken tofu
- 1/4 cup non-fat plain Greek style yogurt
- 1/2 tsp sea salt
- 1/2 tsp Dijon mustard
- 1/2 tsp black pepper
- 1/2 tsp dried oregano
- 2 tsp lemon zest
- 2 tbsp chopped fresh dill
- 1 tbsp fresh thyme leaves

Direction

- Finely mince 2 garlic cloves, set aside.

- Place remaining garlic and water in a small saucepan. Bring to a simmer and cook 5 minutes.
- Reserve 2 tbsp. of the cooking liquid and drain.
- Add all the garlic, tofu, yogurt, salt, mustard, pepper, oregano, lemon zest and reserved cooking liquid into a food processor and puree until completely smooth.
- Scrape into a bowl and fold chopped dill and thyme throughout.
- Chill and stir well before serving.

22. Greek Beet And Potato Salad Recipe

Serving: 6 | Prep: | Cook: | Ready in:

Ingredients

- 1/4 c. salad oil
- 2 tbsp. good wine vinegar or mixture of vinegar & lemon juice
- 1/4 tsp. dry mustard
- fresh ground pepper
- 4 c. diced hot cooked potatoes
- 2 c. diced cooked or canned beets
- 1 med. bermuda onion, finely sliced
- Before serving add:
- 1 tbsp. chopped capers
- 1/4 c. chopped dill pickle
- 1/2 c. ripe olives cut in lg. pieces from pit
- And 1 1/2 cups of one or a mixture of any of the following:
- green peas, cooked
- green beans, diced
- Flaked canned tuna or salmon
- Garnish:optional
- anchovies, green or black olives, parsley sprigs.

Direction

- Prep does not include overnight chilling

- Blend the 4 first ingredients by combining them in a screw top jar and shaking vigorously to blend.
- Pour over the beets, potatoes, onion and peas
- Mix, cover and refrigerate overnight.
- Shortly before serving add: your choice of any peas, beans or tuna or salmon, or just omit
- Then:
- Garnish with

23. Greek Chicken Salad Recipe

Serving: 2 | Prep: | Cook: 20mins | Ready in:

Ingredients

- 2 chicken breasts
- 1 TBS Greek seasoning
- 1/4 cup of olive oil
- juice of 1/2 lemon
- 3 cups of mixed greens
- Assorted veggies (your choice)
- 1/2 cup of extra virgin olive oil
- 2 TBS red wine vinegar
- 1 TBS fresh lemon juice
- 1 tsp salt free Greek seasoning
- 1 tsp honey
- 1 TBS gorgonzola cheese
- 2 TBS feta cheese

Direction

- Combine 1 TBS of Greek seasoning with 1/4 cup of olive oil and the juice of 1/2 lemon. Mix and marinate the chicken at least 4 hrs. or overnight.
- Preheat oven to 350
- In an oven proof skillet on top of the stove over a med-high heat place pan and allow to come up to temp (around 1-2 min)
- Add chicken and sauté for 3 minutes, turn over and repeat for 3 more minutes.
- Place in oven and bake for 15 minutes.
- Remove and allow to rest for 10 minutes.

- Meanwhile place 1/2 cup of extra virgin olive oil in a bowl, the Greek seasoning, red wine vinegar, honey, and lemon juice and whisk for 30 seconds.
- Add the gorgonzola and feta and mash briefly and whisk for 30 seconds.
- Arrange salad then slice chicken into 1/2 in slices and drizzle with vinaigrette.

24. Greek Chicken Orzo Salad Recipe

Serving: 6 | Prep: | Cook: 25mins | Ready in:

Ingredients

- 8 ounces uncooked orzo (pasta)
- 1 can (12 ounces) Italian-herb, diced tomatoes
- 2 tablespoons olive oil
- 1/4 cup chopped fresh mint leaves or 2 tablespoons dried mint
- 2 cloves garlic, minced
- 1 can (10 ounces) white meat chicken, drained
- 1 medium unpeeled cucumber, diced
- 1/4 cup chopped, green onions
- 1/4 cup pitted canned kalamata olives, sliced
- 2 ounces feta cheese, crumbled
- 1 cup shredded, fresh spinach

Direction

- Preparation Time: Approximately 15 minutes
- Cook Time: Approximately 10 minutes
- Preparation:
- Cook orzo according to package directions without oil or salt, until al dente, or tender but firm. Drain and cool under running water.
- Drain tomatoes, reserving liquid. In a small bowl combine reserved liquid from tomatoes, olive oil, mint and garlic; set aside. In a large bowl, combine cooled pasta, with drained tomatoes, chicken, cucumber, green onions, olives and feta cheese. Toss with salad dressing mixture. Chill. Fold in spinach just before serving.

- Servings: 6
- Nutritional Information per Serving:
- Calories 270; Total fat 9g; Saturated fat 3g; Cholesterol 25mg; Sodium 520mg; Carbohydrate 34g; Fiber 2g; Protein 16g; Vitamin A 10%DV*; Vitamin C 15%DV; Calcium 8%DV; Iron 10%DV
- * Daily Value

25. Greek Cucumber Salad Recipe

Serving: 8 | Prep: | Cook: | Ready in:

Ingredients

- 3 large cucumbers, washed with skin on
- 1 cup yoghurt or as needed
- 1 large garlic clove minced
- 1 Tbs fresh minced mint leaves
- salt and pepper to taste
- dash sugar to taste

Direction

- Peel off some strips of the green skin from the cucumber
- Use a fork and score the cucumber with the tines
- Using a mandolin or by hand, cut cukes into almost paper thin or very thin slices
- Place cucumber in a bowl along with minced garlic, minced fresh mint
- Add about 1 cup of yoghurt and mix well.
- Add salt and pepper and a dash of sugar to taste
- Chill.
- Just before serving adjust seasoning if desired
- The yoghurt will become liquidy along with the cukes and this is perfect!
- Serve salad by removing with a slotted spoon

26. Greek Ensalada Recipe

Serving: 6 | Prep: | Cook: | Ready in:

Ingredients

- 2 firm cucumbers, sliced 3/4" thick then quartered
- 2 softball sized tomatoes, cut into chunks size of cukes
- 1 sweet onion, cut up same
- 1/2 block of firm feta cheese, crumbled
- 1/2 pint of pitted kalamata olives
- Dressing:
- 1/3 c. balsamic vinegar
- 1 c. olive oil
- 2 tbsp oregano
- 1 tbsp sweet paprika
- 2 tsp garlic powder
- 1 tsp salt
- ground pepper to taste

Direction

- Mix vegetables together
- Crumble feta over top
- Blend dressing and stir all together
- Refrigerate 20 min. best served cold

27. Greek Green Lentil Salad Recipe

Serving: 4 | Prep: | Cook: | Ready in:

Ingredients

- 8 cups mixed salad greens
- 1/4 red onion sliced
- 1/2 cucumber slicedinto half moons
- 2 tomatoes cut into wedges
- 16 kalamata olives, pitted
- 1 cup cooked green lentils
- feta cheese as neeede to crumble over slalad
- Dressing:
- 1 Tbs Dijon mustard
- 3 tbs red wine vinegar

- 1 clove garlic minced
- salt and pepper to taste

Direction

- Prep does not include the cooking of the lentils!
- Make vinaigrette and place in shaker jar, shake to combine
- Place salad ingredients in a large bowl
- Pour on dressing
- Toss lightly to combine
- Crumble on feta over top
- Serve immediately
- Multiply recipe as needed!

28. Greek Horiatiki Salata Village Salad Recipe

Serving: 4 | Prep: | Cook: | Ready in:

Ingredients

- 2 tomatoes cut in slices
- 1 cucumber (small) cut in slices
- 1 green pepper cut in slices
- 1 onion cut in slices
- 1 spoonful of caper (usually we use the berries but the leaves can be used as well)
- 1/2 table spoonful of dried oregano
- 10 black olives
- feta cheese, cut in pieces
- extra virgin olive oil
- wine vinegar
- salt

Direction

- Wash and cut the vegetables
- Add the olive oils, the caper and all the other ingredients and mix well.

29. Greek Island Dressing Recipe

Serving: 8 | Prep: | Cook: | Ready in:

Ingredients

- Greek Island Dressing
- 1/2 cup cottage cheese
- 1/2 cup crumbled feta cheese
- 1/2 cup milk
- 1 teaspoon grated lemon peel
- 1 teaspoon oregano
- 1 teaspoon freshly ground black pepper

Direction

- In the container of an electric blender combine all ingredients.
- Blend smooth stopping motor and scraping sides as needed.

30. Greek Isle Rice Salad Recipe

Serving: 6 | Prep: | Cook: 30mins | Ready in:

Ingredients

- 1- package of beef- flavor - rice a roni
- 2- tablespoons butter
- 8- ounces thick deli sliced roast beef cut into 1/2 inch pieces
- 1/2- cup chopped red onion
- 1/2- cup sliced black olives
- 3- plum tomatoes, seeded and chopped
- 1/3- cup olive oil
- 1/4- cup lemon juice
- 2- cloves garlic , crushed
- 1/2- teaspoon dried oregano
- 1/2- teaspoon ground black pepper
- 1- medium cucmber, thinly sliced
- 1/2- cup crumbled feta cheese

Direction

- In a large skillet over medium heat, sauté the rice-a-roni with butter until the vermicelli in the rice-a-roni is golden brown
- Slowly stir in 2 1/2- cups water and special seasonings and bring to a boil
- Reduce heat to low simmer 15 to 20 minutes- or until the rice is tender. Cool completely
- In a large bowl, combine olive oil, lemon juice, garlic, oregano, and pepper, with a wire whisk.
- Toss rice mixture with dressing.
- Chill at least 30 minutes
- Garnish with cucumber slices and feta cheese

31. Greek Mushroom Salad Recipe

Serving: 4 | Prep: | Cook: 10mins |Ready in:

Ingredients

- 1 Tablespoon olive oil
- 1/2 pound fresh cremini, button, and shiitake mushrooms, sliced and trimmed
- 3 cloves garlic, chopped fine
- 1 teaspoon dried basil or dried marjoram
- 1 medium tomato, diced
- 3 Tablespoons lemon juice
- 1/2 cup of water
- Pinch of salt
- Pinch of fresh ground pepper
- 1 Tablespoon fresh chopped parsley or fresh coriander

Direction

- Heat the oil on low in a frying pan, then gently fry the mushrooms for 2-3 minutes.
- Do not overcook.
- Sprinkle in garlic and basil, then toss the mixture for a minute or two so that mushrooms are well coated.
- Add the tomato, lemon juice, water, salt, and pepper.
- Stir together and cook until the tomato softens.

- Remove from heat and let cool.
- Garnish with chopped herbs.

32. Greek Octopus Salad Recipe

Serving: 4 | Prep: | Cook: 60mins |Ready in:

Ingredients

- 1 octopus fresh or frozen (about 1 kilo)
- ½ glass of white dry wine
- ½ glass of olive oil
- A few peppercorns
- 3 – 4 bay leaves
- 2 medium potatoes
- 2- 3 spring onions
- parsley
- salt and pepper
- oregano (optional)
- lemon juice

Direction

- Put the octopus with the sac in the sauce pan (do not cut it into pieces) and let it boil, lower heat and turn it on the other side as well.
- Place lid on pan and simmer for about half an hour or more (fresh octopus needs more time than the frozen one to tenderize). A pinkish to red liquid will sweat out of the octopus which, after half an hour or so, through away. Add the olive oil, the wine, bay leaves and peppercorns in the sauce pan (no salt) and when it begins boiling lower heat and simmer until the octopus becomes tender (about half an hour again).
- Meantime bake potatoes with skin either in the oven or cook in the microwave until soft. Sometimes I place them in the basket of the pressure cooker (again with skin) and steam them for about 15 minutes.
- When they can be handled, peel and cut them into small pieces. Finely chop the onions and parsley and mix with the potatoes. Add the sauce of the octopus which you have reserved

and mix all together as well as extra olive oil, lemon, salt, pepper and oregano, at will.

33. Greek Orzo Salad Recipe

Serving: 6 | Prep: | Cook: 8mins | Ready in:

Ingredients

- 1 1/2 cups uncooked orzo pasta
- 2 (6 ounce) cans marinated artichoke hearts
- 1 tomato, seeded and chopped
- 1 cucumber, seeded and chopped
- 1 red onion, chopped
- 1 cup crumbled feta cheese
- 1 (2 ounce) can black olives, drained
- 1/4 cup chopped fresh parsley
- 1 tablespoon lemon juice
- 1/2 teaspoon dried oregano
- 1/2 teaspoon lemon pepper

Direction

- Bring a large pot of lightly salted water to a boil.
- Add pasta and cook for 8 to 10 minutes or until al dente; drain.
- Drain artichoke hearts, reserving liquid.
- In large bowl combine pasta, artichoke hearts, tomato, cucumber, onion, feta, olives, parsley, lemon juice, oregano and lemon pepper.
- Toss and chill for 1 hour in refrigerator.
- Just before serving, drizzle reserved artichoke marinade over salad

34. Greek Pasta Recipe

Serving: 4 | Prep: | Cook: 15mins | Ready in:

Ingredients

- 8 oz. whole wheat penne pasta
- 8 ounces boneless, skinless chicken, chopped

- 16 calamata olives
- 1 cup reduced fat feta cheese crumbles
- 3 cloves garlic, minced
- 1.5 cup whole mushrooms
- 1 cup cherry tomatoes, halved
- 1 tbsp balsamic vinegar

Direction

- Cook pasta. In a separate pan, cook chicken and garlic in balsamic vinegar. When chicken is cooked thoroughly, add mushrooms and tomatoes to heat.
- Mix cooked pasta, chicken, garlic and mushrooms. Add olives and top with feta crumbles.
- This meal could easily become vegetarian by omitting chicken. Add onion or peppers for a twist.

35. Greek Pasta Salad Recipe

Serving: 6 | Prep: | Cook: 10mins | Ready in:

Ingredients

- 1 package (12 oz) colored corkscrew pasta
- 1 cucumber thinly seeded and sliced thinly
- 1 cup crumbled feta cheese
- 1/2 cup olive oil
- 1/2 cup sliced black or Greek olives
- 2 tablespoon lemon juice
- 1/2 cup sliced radishes
- 2 tablespoon chopped fresh parsley
- 1/4 cup sliced green onions
- 1-2 cloves minced garlic
- 1 teaspoon oregano

Direction

- In large bowl toss hot cooked pasta, cheese, olives, radishes, onions and cucumber until they are well mixed. In small bowl or jar combine the rest of ingredients. Toss with pasta until evenly coated with 2/3 of the dressing. Chill salad 1-2 hours. Toss with remaining dressing just before serving.

36. Greek Potato Salad Recipe

Serving: 8 | Prep: | Cook: 20mins | Ready in:

Ingredients

- 3 lbs. red bliss potatoes,cut in small pieces or sliced
- 1 lg. red onion,sliced thin
- 1 small can black olives,sliced
- 2 TB red wine vinegar
- 1/4-1/2 c mayonnaise
- 3 TB olive oil
- salt and pepper to taste

Direction

- Boil potatoes till tender...let cool. Mix potatoes with mayo, vinegar, oil, salt, peer, onions and olives. Toss till lightly coated. If you prefer salad more moist, add more mayo, vinegar and oil.
- As I mentioned, I add crumbled feta and sometimes chopped cucumber.

37. Greek Potato Salad With Dried Tomatoes Recipe

Serving: 4 | Prep: | Cook: 30mins | Ready in:

Ingredients

- 1 pound potatoes cut into 1/4" slices
- 1 cup dried tomato halves
- lemon Dressing:
- 1/4 cup olive oil
- 1/4 cup water
- 2-1/2 tablespoons lemon juice
- 1 large garlic clove pressed
- 1 tablespoon chopped fresh oregano

- 1 teaspoon salt
- 1/2 teaspoon freshly ground black pepper
- 1 cup sliced seedless cucumbers
- 1/2 cup sliced red onion
- 1 cup crumbled feta cheese
- 1/2 cup Greek olives

Direction

- Cook potatoes covered in 2" boiling water 12 minutes then drain well and set aside.
- Meanwhile in small bowl cover tomatoes with boiling water then set aside.
- Thoroughly drain tomatoes and pat dry with paper towels.
- In large bowl whish together all dressing ingredients.
- Add potatoes, tomatoes and cucumbers to bowl containing dressing then toss to coat.
- Mound potato mixture on plate and arrange onion, cheese and olives on top.

38. Greek Potato And Chickpea Salad Recipe

Serving: 6 | Prep: | Cook: 15mins | Ready in:

Ingredients

- **Dressing **
- 2 tbsp cold vegetable broth
- 2 tbsp lemon juice
- 1 tsp grated lemon zest
- 1 tbsp Dijon mustard
- **Salad**
- 1lb red-skinned new potatoes, scrubbed, quartered and steamed
- 1 large red onion, thinly sliced
- 15oz cooked chickpeas, rinsed and drained
- 6oz cherry tomatoes, halved
- 2oz black olives, pitted & chopped
- 3 tbsp fresh oregano, chopped

Direction

- Whisk together the dressing ingredients in a small bowl, set aside.
- Put the potatoes into a bowl.
- While still warm, pour half of the dressing over them and toss.
- Cool to room temperature.
- Add the onion, chickpeas, tomatoes, olives & oregano.
- Pour on the remaining dressing, toss together and serve at room temperature.

39. Greek Ramen Salad Recipe

Serving: 1 | Prep: | Cook: 3mins | Ready in:

Ingredients

- 2 Cups of water
- 2 Packages of ramen noodles
- 1 Cup feta cheese, cut into chunks
- 1 Cup red peppers, cut into small pieces
- 1/2 Cup onions, cut into small pieces
- 1/2 Cup black olives, cut into small pieces
- 1/2 Cup green olives, cut into small pieces
- 1/2 Cup of tomatoes, cut into small pieces
- 1/2 Cup of canola oil
- 1/2 Cup of onions, cut into small pieces
- 1/4 Cup of citrus juice
- salt and pepper

Direction

- Bring 2 cups of water to a boil. Add your ramen noodles.
- Wait 2-3 minutes until the noodles are tender and separated. Drain
- Mix the canola oil and the citrus juice in a bowl.
- Add some salt and pepper.
- Add the chopped vegetables and feta cheese on top of your noodles.
- Pour the dressing over the salad and serve.

40. Greek Salad Dressing 2 Recipe

Serving: 4 | Prep: | Cook: | Ready in:

Ingredients

- 2 tablespoons lemon juice
- 3 tablespoon water
- 1 minced garlic cloves
- 1 teaspoon dried thyme leaves
- 1 teaspoon dried Greek oregano leaves
- 1 teaspoon anchovy paste or mashed anchovies
- 1/4 teaspoon salt
- 1/4 teaspoon black cracked pepper
- 3/4 cup extra virgin olive oil

Direction

- Put lemon juice into a shaker bottle. Add water and the other ingredients, except the olive oil. Stir well to blend the dry ingredients into the wet. Add olive oil and shake thoroughly.
- Shake prior to each use.
- Keep in refrigerator

41. Greek Salad Dressing 3 Recipe

Serving: 4 | Prep: | Cook: | Ready in:

Ingredients

- 2 tablespoons balsamic vinegar
- 2 tablespoon water
- 1/2 teaspoon dried thyme leaves
- 1/2 teaspoon dried Greek oregano leaves
- 1/2 teaspoon dried crushed basil leaves
- 1/2 teaspoon dried marjoram leaves
- 1/4 teaspoon salt
- 1/4 teaspoon black cracked pepper
- 3/4 cup extra virgin olive oil

Direction

- Put vinegar into a shaker bottle. Add water and the other ingredients, except the olive oil. Stir well to blend the dry ingredients into the wet.
- Add olive oil and shake thoroughly. Shake prior to each use.
- Keep in refrigerator

42. Greek Salad Recipe

Serving: 25 | Prep: | Cook: 10mins | Ready in:

Ingredients

- 1 Carton cherry tomatoes
- 1 Cup Pitted kalamata olives
- 1 cucumber
- 1/2 Cup Crumbled feta
- 1 Cup Greek Dressing

Direction

- 1. Preheat oven to 400 degrees. Toss the tomatoes and olives with 1/3 a cup of the Greek salad dressing and then drop on a cookie sheet pan. Bake for 30 minutes or until the tomatoes start to crack and wilt.
- 2. Slice your cucumber into ½ inch thick slices.
- 3. To assemble, place cucumber slice on the serving platter, then smear one roasted tomato on top, one olive, a few crumbles of feta on top, and then drizzle the whole plate with the extra Greek salad dressing.

43. Greek Salad Recipe Recipe

Serving: 4 | Prep: | Cook: | Ready in:

Ingredients

- 200g feta cheese, diced
- 500g fresh tomatoes, diced
- 500g cucumbers, diced

- 1 red onion, medium, thinly sliced
- 1 green bell pepper, sliced
- 100g black olives
- 80ml olive oil
- 40ml red wine vinegar (optional)
- 1 tbsp oregano
- salt to taste

Direction

- Wash and cut all vegetables as indicated.
- Combine feta cheese, tomato, cucumber, onion, black olives and pepper in a salad bowl.
- Combine olive oil and vinegar in a jar, close tightly and shake well.
- Pour over salad and season with salt to taste. Sprinkle with oregano and serve.

44. Greek Salad Skewers Recipe

Serving: 4 | Prep: | Cook: 10mins | Ready in:

Ingredients

- One-quarter english cucumber
- kosher salt and freshly ground black pepper
- 1/4 lb. feta cheese, cut into 16 small cubes
- 8 pitted kalamata olives, halved
- 8 ripe grape or cherry tomatoes, halved
- 2 Tbs. extra-virgin olive oil

Direction

- Cut four 1/2-inch-thick diagonal slices from the cucumber and then quarter each slice.
- Set the cucumber pieces on a large serving platter and season with 1/4 tsp. each salt and pepper.
- Top each with a piece of feta and then an olive half.
- Stab a toothpick through a tomato half and then thread through one of the cucumber stacks, pushing the toothpick down to secure it.

- Drizzle with the olive oil, sprinkle with some more black pepper, and serve.
- These keep at room temperature for up to 1 hour before serving.
- From Fine Cooking

45. Greek Salad Vinaigrette Recipe

Serving: 4 | Prep: | Cook: | Ready in:

Ingredients

- 1/4 cup red wine vinegar
- 1 minced garlic clove
- 2 tablespoons minced fresh parsley leaves
- 1 teaspoon dried Greek oregano leaves
- 1/4 teaspoon salt
- 1/4 teaspoon black cracked pepper
- 2/3 cup extra virgin olive oil

Direction

- Put vinegar into a shaker bottle. Add the other ingredients, except the olive oil. Stir well to blend the dry ingredients into the wet. Add olive oil and shake thoroughly.
- Shake prior to each use.
- Keep in refrigerator

46. Greek Shrimp Pasta Salad Recipe

Serving: 12 | Prep: | Cook: 10mins | Ready in:

Ingredients

- 1 lb. small pasta shells
- 1 lb. cooked salad shrimp
- 1 C. EVOO
- ¼ C. wine vinegar
- ¼ C. lemon juice
- 1 T. fresh, minced thyme

- 3 garlic cloves, minced
- 1 lb. fresh tomatoes, chopped
- 1 C. kalamata olives, quartered
- 1 large bell pepper, chopped
- 1 C. marinated artichoke hearts, drained and chopped
- 6 oz feta cheese, crumbled
- 6 green onions, chopped

Direction

- Cook pasta according to package. Drain and rinse with cold water.
- Mix the EVOO, vinegar, lemon juice, thyme, garlic and pepper, set aside.
- When pasta is cool, place in large bowl add remaining ingredients and toss with dressing.

47. Greek Spinach Salad Recipe

Serving: 6 | Prep: | Cook: | Ready in:

Ingredients

- 2 bunches spinach
- 1/2 cup red onion thinly sliced
- 1/2 cup peeled and seeded cucumbers thinly sliced
- 1/2 cup sliced radishes
- 4 ounces feta cheese crumbled
- 1 teaspoon Dijon mustard
- 2 tablespoons chopped parsley
- 1 green onion sliced
- 1 tablespoon lemon juice
- 1 teaspoon minced garlic
- 2 tablespoons olive oil
- 1/4 cup pine nuts for garnish
- 1/4 cup Greek olives for garnish

Direction

- Wash spinach then remove stems and pat leaves dry and tear into bite size pieces.
- Place spinach in a salad bowl with red onion, cucumbers, radishes and half of the feta.

- In a blender puree remaining feta, mustard, parsley, green onion, lemon juice, garlic and oil.
- Pour over salad then garnish with pine nuts and Greek olives.

48. Greek Style Pasta Salad With Feta Recipe

Serving: 4 | Prep: | Cook: 25mins | Ready in:

Ingredients

- 1 red bell pepper, chopped
- 1 yellow bell pepper, chopped
- 1/2 english cucumber, chopped
- 1 medium eggplant, cubed
- 1 small zucchini, cut in 1/4 inch slices
- 6 tbsp olive oil
- 4 pc sundried tomatoes, soaked in 1/2 cup boiling water
- 1/2 c torn arugula leaves
- 1/2 c chopped fresh basil
- 2 tbsp balsamic vinegar
- 2 tbsp minced garlic
- 4 oz crumbled feta cheese
- 1 (12 oz) package bowtie pasta
- salt and pepper

Direction

- Preheat oven to 450 degrees.
- In a bowl toss the peppers, eggplant, and zucchini with 2 tablespoons of the olive oil, salt, and pepper.
- Arrange on the prepared cookie sheet and bake vegetables for 25 minutes in the preheated oven until lightly browned.
- Salt and pepper veggies once they are out of the oven.
- In the meantime put a large pot of salted boiling water, cook pasta 10 to 12 minutes, until al dente, and drain.
- Drain the softened sun-dried tomatoes and reserve the water.

- In a large bowl, toss together the roasted vegetables, cooked pasta, sun-drained tomatoes, arugula, cucumber and basil.
- Mix in remaining olive oil, reserved water from tomatoes, balsamic vinegar, garlic, and feta cheese; toss to coat.
- Season with salt and pepper to taste.

49. Greek Style Potato Salad Recipe

Serving: 8 | Prep: | Cook: 15mins | Ready in:

Ingredients

- 1 lb potatoes, peeled, cut into bit sized pieces
- 2 scallions finely chopped
- 10 (+) kalamata olives, pitted and halved
- 2 tspn capers
- 3 - 4 oz. feta cheese, crumbled
- 1 Tbsp finely chopped fresh dill
- 1 Tbsp EVOO (olive oil)
- 1 Tbsp lemon juice or juice from 1/2 fresh lemon.
- 1/2 tspn sugar
- 1/4 cup Greek style yogurt
- 1/2 tspn sea salt
- 1/4 tspn fresh ground pepper

Direction

- Boil potatoes in a large pot of boiling water. Cook until tender.
- Drain potatoes, allow to cool.
- In a small bowl, dissolve sugar in the lemon juice. Mix together with the olive oil, yogurt, salt, and pepper until well combined.
- Place cooked potatoes in large bowl, scatter the scallions, capers, olives, feta cheese, and dill on top and toss gently to combine.
- Drizzle the yogurt dressing over the top, mix to evenly coat the potatoes.
- Serve…. and enjoy.

50. Greek Style Salad Recipe

Serving: 4 | Prep: | Cook: | Ready in:

Ingredients

- 3 romaine lettuce leaves
- 1 medium tomato
- 1/4 cup feta cheese crumbled
- Dressing:
- 1/2 tablespoon olive oil
- 1/2 tablespoon lemon juice
- 1/4 teaspoon oregano
- 1/4 teaspoon garlic salt
- 1/8 teaspoon thyme
- 1/8 teaspoon freshly ground black pepper
- 6 pitted black olives

Direction

- Tear lettuce into bite size pieces and cut tomato into small chunks.
- In glass bowl combine lettuce, tomato and cheese then cover and chill.
- In a cup combine olive oil, lemon juice, spices and beat together with a fork.
- Pour dressing over salad and toss gently to coat ingredients.
- Slice olives and sprinkle over salad then serve immediately.

51. Greek Summer Salad Recipe

Serving: 2 | Prep: | Cook: 10mins | Ready in:

Ingredients

- 1 medium size cucumber
- 1 medium size onion
- 1 medium size tomatoe
- 1 small green pepper
- few olives (opt)
- 100 gm feta cheese
- olive oil
- 1 tsp of vinegar
- salt n oregano for taste

Direction

- Wash n clean all the vegetables ... peel the cucumber roughly chop all the vegetables n add it in a salad bowl.... add very good amount of olive oil some salt to taste n vinegar mix it well ... then add feta cheese on the top and drizzle it with some olive oil again.... sprinkle oregano on the top of the feta cheese....
- Done!!!! Serve with some bread....
- Enjoy!!!
- Tip: I always prefer not to peel cucumber but it's opt and up to you...
- You can add some olives or some kapari if available....
- Bread is always served with salad as Greeks love to dip bread pieces in the salad oil ....try it u will love it too!!!!
- Here in Greece we have different kind of feta in which some are salty so we don't add salt to the salad ....but it totally depends on the feta available at your place... I personally love to crumble feta in the salad ... but usually a small title of feta is served with salad ....it's up to u again

52. Greek Tomato Salad Recipe

Serving: 6 | Prep: | Cook: | Ready in:

Ingredients

- 5 ripe large tomatoes, cut into 1/3-inch-thick rounds
- 1 small red onion, thinly sliced
- 1/4 cup extra-virgin olive oil
- 1 tablespoon balsamic vinegar
- 4 ounces feta cheese, crumbled
- 1/4 cup kalamata olives or other brine-cured black olives, pitted
- 1 tablespoon chopped fresh parsley

Direction

- Arrange tomatoes on platter. Top with onion slices. Mix oil and vinegar and drizzle over tomatoes and onions. Sprinkle with salt and pepper to taste. Let stand at room temperature at least 1 hour. Sprinkle cheese, olives and parsley over salad and serve.

53. Greek Tomatoes Recipe

Serving: 4 | Prep: | Cook: |Ready in:

Ingredients

- 3 medium tomatoes, cut in eighths
- 3 tablespoons olive oil
- 2 tablespoons balsamic vinegar
- 1 Tablespoon Greek seasoning Mix

Direction

- Boil a pan of water, place a tomato in the boiling water for about 10 seconds. Remove and the skin will peel off effortlessly.
- Cut the tomatoes vertically into 8 wedges each.
- Place in a bowl with the other ingredients. Toss gently to coat. Let stand for 15 minutes before serving.

54. Greek Tortellini Salad Recipe

Serving: 6 | Prep: | Cook: 20mins |Ready in:

Ingredients

- 2 (9 ounce) packages cheese tortellini
- 1/2 cup extra virgin olive oil
- 1/4 cup lemon juice
- 1/4 cup red wine vinegar
- 2 tablespoons chopped fresh parsley
- 1 teaspoon dried oregano

- 1/2 teaspoon salt
- 6 eggs
- 1 pound baby spinach leaves
- 1 cup crumbled feta cheese
- 1/2 cup slivered red onion

Direction

- Prep time does not include chill time
- Bring a large pot of lightly salted water to a boil.
- Add tortellini, and cook for 7 minutes or until al dente; drain.
- In a large bowl, mix the olive oil, lemon juice, red wine vinegar, parsley, oregano, and salt.
- Place the cooked tortellini in the bowl, and toss to coat.
- Cover, and chill at least 2 hours in the refrigerator.
- Place eggs in a saucepan with enough water to cover, and bring to a boil.
- Remove from heat, and allow eggs to sit in the hot water for 10 to 12 minutes.
- Drain, cool, peel, and quarter.
- Gently mix the spinach, feta cheese, and onion into the bowl with the pasta.
- Arrange the quartered eggs around the salad to serve.

55. Greek Veggie Salad Recipe

Serving: 2 | Prep: | Cook: |Ready in:

Ingredients

- 1 cucumber, peeled,seeded and diced
- 1 large tomato, diced
- 1 red pepper, diced
- 1 scallion, finely sliced or minced
- 2 tablespoons minced fresh parsley
- 2 tablespoons extra-virgin olive oil
- juice of 1/2 a lemon (or more to taste)
- 1 garlic clove, pressed
- 1/4 tsp dried oregano

- 8 black Calamata olives, whole or pitted and sliced
- salt and pepper to taste
- crumbed or grated feta cheese (whatever amount you like)

Direction

- Combine the cucumbers, tomatoes, bell peppers, scallion (or red onion), oil, lemon juice, garlic, oregano and olives in a large bowl. Add salt and pepper, and toss well. Sprinkle feta on salad when ready to serve.
- Even though you can serve this salad immediately, it is nice if it sits in the fridge for 30 minutes before serving.

56. Greek Yogurt Ranch Dressing And Spinach Salad Recipe

Serving: 4 | Prep: | Cook: |Ready in:

Ingredients

- 1/4 cup Greek yoghurt
- 1 Tbs honey
- 1/4 cup buttermilk
- juice of 1/2 lemon
- salt and pepper to taste
- Salad:
- 6 cups spinach leaves
- 2 sliced nectarines
- 1/2 c crumbled feta cheese
- 1/4 crushed walnuts

Direction

- Whisk all.
- Chill 30 minutes
- Serve over a salad composed of spinach leaves, sliced nectarines crumbled feta cheese and some crushed walnuts
- Multiply dressing as needed

57. Greek Lamb And Cucumber Salad With Yogurt Dressing Recipe

Serving: 4 | Prep: | Cook: 14mins |Ready in:

Ingredients

- 2 teaspoons snipped fresh rosemary or 1/2 teaspoon dried rosemary, crushed
- 1 clove garlic, minced
- 8 ounces boneless lamb leg sirloin chops, cut 1/2 inch thick
- 8 cups torn fresh spinach or torn mixed salad greens
- 1 15-ounce can garbanzo beans, rinsed and drained
- 1/4 cup chopped, seeded cucumber
- 1/2 cup plain low-fat yogurt
- 1/4 cup chopped green onions
- 1/8 to 1/4 teaspoon salt
- 1/8 teaspoon pepper
- 1 clove garlic, minced
- 1/4 cup dried tart cherries or golden raisins

Direction

- Combine rosemary and 1 clove garlic; rub evenly onto lamb chops. Place chops on the unheated rack of a broiler pan. Broil 4 to 5 inches from the heat for 12 to 15 minutes, turning once halfway through.
- Or use grill for 14 minutes.
- Cut lamb chops into thin bite-size slices.
- Meanwhile, in a large bowl toss together spinach, garbanzo beans, and cucumber.
- Divide spinach mixture among 4 plates. Arrange lamb slices atop spinach mixture.
- For dressing, in a small bowl combine yogurt, green onions, salt, pepper, and 1 clove garlic.
- Drizzle dressing over salads.
- Sprinkle with cherries or raisins.
- *Note: If desired, grill chops on the rack of an uncovered grill directly over medium coals to desired doneness, turning once halfway

through. (Allow 10 to 14 minutes for medium-rare or 14 to 16 minutes for medium

58. Greek Style Shrimp Salad Recipe

Serving: 4 | Prep: | Cook: | Ready in:

Ingredients

- 3/4 cup chopped kalamata olives
- 1/2 cup basil leaves
- 3 tablespoons finely chopped red onion
- 3 tablespoons fresh lemon juice
- 1 1/2 tablespoons olive oil
- 1 pound small shrimp, cooked and peeled
- 1 bag of mixed salad greens
- 2 diced plum tomatoes
- 1/4 cup dried or fresh parsley
- Freshly ground black pepper, to taste
- Your favorite rustic bread loaf, sliced

Direction

- Put the first 5 ingredients in a blender or food processor, and pulse several times to create a rough paste.
- Put 1/2 cup of the paste mixture in a large bowl.
- Add shrimp, then toss to coat.
- Add remaining paste mixture to the salad greens then toss to coat.
- Place the greens equally onto 4 plates, and top with shrimp mixture,
- Then sprinkle with the tomato.
- Garnish with parsley and pepper.
- Serve with bread.

59. Greek Style Tuna Salad Recipe

Serving: 6 | Prep: | Cook: 15mins | Ready in:

Ingredients

- 1 cup orzo, uncooked
- 1 (61/8) can solid white tuna, drained and flaked
- 2 cups chopped tomato
- 1/2 cup crumbled feta cheese
- 1/4 cup chopped purple onion
- 3 Tbs sliced ripe olives
- 1/2 cup red wine vinegar
- 2 Tbs water
- 2 Tbs olive oil
- 1 clove garlic, minced
- 1/2 tsp dried basil
- 1/2 tsp dried oregano
- green leaf lettuce (optional)

Direction

- Cook orzo according to package directions; drain rinse with cold water and drain again
- Combine orzo, tuna, tomato, feta, onion and olives in a large bowl
- Toss gently
- Combine vinegar, water, olive oil, garlic, basil and oregano in container of an electric blender;
- Cover and process until smooth, stopping once to scrape down sides.
- Pour vinegar mixture over pasta mixture and toss gently.
- Cover and chill thoroughly,
- Serve on lettuce leaves if desired.

60. Greek Tacular Pasta Salad Recipe

Serving: 10 | Prep: | Cook: 10mins | Ready in:

Ingredients

- 2 1/2 cups uncooked farfalle pasta
- 1 cup greek dressing
- 2 1/2 tbs mayonnaise
- 4 radishes, finely chopped

- 1/2 cucumber, peeled & chopped
- 1 15oz can chick peas, drained
- 3/4 cup crumbled feta cheese

Direction

- Bring a medium pot of salted water to a boil. Add farfalle & cook until al dente, then strain & place in medium sized bowl.
- Stir in the Greek dressing & mayonnaise until farfalle is well coated. Fold in radishes, cucumbers, chick peas & feta. Cover & chill until ready for serving.

61. Grilled Eggplant And Feta Salad Recipe

Serving: 4 | Prep: | Cook: 15mins | Ready in:

Ingredients

- 3 tablespoons olive oil with 1 crushed clove of garlic
- 2 eggplants, ends trimmed, cut into 1-inch wide slices
- 1/2 cup toasted pine nuts
- 1/2 cup ounces feta, crumbled
- 1/3 cup basil, thinly sliced
- 2 tablespoons chopped mint
- 3 tablespoons extra-virgin olive oil
- 3 tablespoons balsamic vinegar
- 1/2 teaspoon kosher salt
- 1/2 teaspoon freshly ground black pepper

Direction

- Preheat a gas or charcoal grill. Brush the garlic flavored olive oil over the slices of eggplant and season with salt & pepper. Grill the eggplants until tender and grill marks appear, about 3 to 4 minutes per side.
- Place the eggplants side-by-side on a serving platter. Sprinkle with the pine nuts, feta cheese, basil, and mint. Drizzle with extra-virgin olive oil, balsamic vinegar.

62. Grilled Vegetable Salad Recipe Recipe

Serving: 4 | Prep: | Cook: | Ready in:

Ingredients

- 2 eggplants, thickly sliced
- 80g oyster mushrooms
- 2 red bell peppers, quartered lengthways
- 2 yellow bell peppers, quartered lengthways
- 2 courgettes, thickly sliced
- 150ml olive oil
- 1 tbsp oregano
- 80g hazelnuts roasted, coarsely chopped
- 1 bunch lettuce, torn into pieces
- salt and black pepper to taste
- Vinaigrette Dressing
- 100ml olive oil
- 50ml red wine vinegar
- 1 tsp French mustard
- salt and white pepper to taste

Direction

- Wash and cut all vegetables as indicated.
- Brush eggplant, mushrooms, peppers and courgettes with olive oil and cook under a hot grill.
- Place lettuce in a large bowl and drizzle with some of the vinaigrette.
- Season with salt and pepper to taste and arrange on a salad platter.
- Top with grilled vegetables and remaining vinaigrette and garnish with hazelnut pieces.
- To prepare vinaigrette dressing combine all ingredients in a jar, close tightly and shake well until completely mixed.

63. Health Ceasar Salad Dressing Recipe

Serving: 4 | Prep: | Cook: 15mins | Ready in:

Ingredients

- 1/3 cup low-fat or nonfat Greek-style yogurt
- 2 anchovy fillets, mashed
- 1 garlic clove, minced
- 2 tablespoons fresh lemon juice
- 2 teaspoons Worcestershire sauce
- 2 tablespoons extra-virgin olive oil
- 1/4 cup freshly grated Parmigiano-Reggiano cheese
- Salt and freshly ground pepper
- 1 large head of romaine lettuce, torn into bite-size pieces

Direction

- 1. In a small bowl, whisk the yogurt with the anchovies, garlic, lemon juice and Worcestershire sauce. Whisk in the oil and half of the cheese and season with salt and pepper.
- 2. In a large bowl, toss the romaine with half the dressing and the remaining cheese. Serve, passing the remaining dressing at the table.

64. Herbed Greek Chicken Salad Recipe

Serving: 4 | Prep: | Cook: | Ready in:

Ingredients

- 1 teaspoon dried oregano
- 1/2 teaspoon garlic powder
- 3/4 teaspoon black pepper, divided
- 1/2 teaspoon salt, divided
- cooking spray
- 1 pound skinless, boneless chicken breast, cut into 1-inch cubes
- 5 teaspoons fresh lemon juice, divided
- 1 cup plain fat-free yogurt

- 2 teaspoons tahini (sesame-seed paste)
- 1 teaspoon bottled minced garlic
- 8 cups chopped romaine lettuce
- 1 cup peeled chopped english cucumber
- 1 cup grape tomatoes, halved
- 6 pitted kalamata olives, halved
- 1/4 cup (1 ounce) crumbled feta cheese

Direction

- Combine oregano, garlic powder, 1/2 teaspoon pepper, and 1/4 teaspoon salt in a bowl. Heat a non-stick skillet over medium-high heat. Coat pan with cooking spray. Add chicken and spice mixture; sauté until chicken is done. Drizzle with 1 tablespoon juice; stir. Remove from pan.
- Combine remaining 2 teaspoons juice, remaining 1/4 teaspoon salt, remaining 1/4 teaspoon pepper, yogurt, tahini, and garlic in a small bowl; stir well. Combine lettuce, cucumber, tomatoes, and olives. Place 2 1/2 cups of lettuce mixture on each of 4 plates. Top each serving with 1/2 cup chicken mixture and 1 tablespoon cheese. Drizzle each serving with 3 tablespoons yogurt mixture.
- Serve with Toasted Pita Wedges.

65. Horiatiki Greek Salad Recipe

Serving: 4 | Prep: | Cook: | Ready in:

Ingredients

- 4 tomatoes sliced in segments
- 1 medium red onion sliced
- 1/2 sliced cucumber
- 1/8 cup olive oil
- 1/4 cup sliced feta cheese
- 1/4 teaspoon salt
- 1/2 teaspoon freshly ground black pepper
- 2 tablespoons fresh ground oregano chopped
- 1 cup green olives sliced

Direction

- Combine tomatoes, onion, cucumber, olive oil and feta cheese and mix well.
- Sprinkle olives over top then season with salt, pepper and oregano.

66. Horiatiki Salata (greek Salad) Recipe

Serving: 0 | Prep: | Cook: 30mins | Ready in:

Ingredients

- 4-5 ripe tomatoes, in chunks
- 1 large red onion, thinly sliced
- 1 cucumber, sliced
- 1 green bell pepper, sliced into rings
- 1/4 lb of greek feta cheese (crumbled)
- oregano
- sea salt
- olive oil
- 1 dozen green olives (kalamata)
- peppercini

Direction

- Put everything in bowl, sprinkle with the oregano, pour olive oil over salad and toss. Place feta on top and toss into the salad and drizzle with the olive oil and garnish with olives

67. Horitaki Greek Salad Recipe

Serving: 4 | Prep: | Cook: | Ready in:

Ingredients

- 4 tomatoes sliced in segments
- 1 large red onion sliced
- 1/2 sliced cucumber
- 2 tablespoons olive oil
- 1/4 cup feta cheese

- 1/2 teaspoon salt
- 1/2 teaspoon oregano
- 1 teaspoon freshly ground black pepper

Direction

- Combine all ingredients except olive oil and toss gently. Spread olive oil over all and sprinkle with salt, pepper and oregano.

68. In An Octopus's Garden Χταπόδι Στη Σχάρα Recipe

Serving: 4 | Prep: | Cook: 6hours | Ready in:

Ingredients

- 4 lbs. of baby octopi (about 3 of them)
- 2 large lemons
- 1 cup of red wine vinegar (cheap stuff is OK)
- 8 bay leaves
- 3 tbls. of black peppercorns
- 3 gallons of water
- ---MARINADE---
- 1 cup of olive oil
- The juice of 3 lemons
- 2 oz. of ouzo or tsipouro
- 6 cloves of minced garlic
- 1/3 oz. of fresh oregano
- --- UNDER THE SEA SALSA---
- 1 large green bell pepper
- 1 large purple bell pepper
- 1 cup of brine cured kalamata olives
- Half a cucumber
- 3 oz. of finely crumbled feta cheese
- Half a bunch of fresh cilantro
- 3 tbls. of fresh mint
- 2 tsp. of red pepper flakes
- 1/3 cup of olive oil
- The juice of two lemons
- salt
- ---SALAD---
- 2 medium sized aubergines
- 2 tender young zucchinis

- 3 red bell peppers
- 1 bunch of smaller sized asparagus
- 4 cups of baby spinach
- pita bread (cut in fourths)
- olive oil, salt and black pepper
- Your favourite Greek vinaigrette

Direction

- FOR THE OCTOPUS: Rinse it well and clean it removing the ink sack, eyes and other displeasantries. Slice the lemons and put them into a large pot filled with the water and with the vinegar, bay leaves and peppercorns. Bring to a boil. Add the octopi whole and reduce the heat to all but a simmer. Cook gently for 30 minutes then drain and cool.
- When cool, further clean it by taking off the membranous skin. Separate the tentacles and slice the head into thick strips. Set it into the marinade for 6 hours.
- Cook it upon a charcoal grill and a little smoke-wood wouldn't hurt.
- FOR THE SALSA: De-seed the cucumber, and with the peel still on chop it finely. Chop the peppers a little larger and finely chop the herbs. The olives need only be roughly chopped. Mix in the cheese and the pepper flakes and dress with the oil and lemon juice. Season with the salt.
- FOR THE SALAD: Cut all the vegetables into pristine sizes and shapes but not too thickly. Lightly toss them in olive oil and season with salt and pepper. Cook them likewise on the charcoal grill.
- When finished put the lot of them into a bowl, add the spinach and toss in the Greek vinaigrette. This may be a good time to mention that the pita bread should have been oiled and grilled too.
- SERVE: Divide the salad into four portions in the center of some suitable plates. Divide the octopus similarly and set it on top. Garnish the top with the salsa and the wedges of the bread along the border of the plate.

69. Jimmy's Special Salad Recipe

Serving: 4 | Prep: | Cook: 10mins | Ready in:

Ingredients

- Salad
- 2 cups chopped romaine lettuce
- 1 cup diced tomato
- 1 cup diced Persian cucumber
- 1 cup diced celery
- 1 cup carrots, diced or sliced
- 1/2 cup diced red onion
- 1/2 cup pepperoncini (mild), sliced
- 1/2 cup kalamata olives, quartered (+pitted)
- 2 tbsp fresh dill, chopped
- 1 cup feta, crumbled
- *Add pickled beets if you like, about 1/2 - 1 cup, chopped
- Dressing
- 1/2 cup olive oil
- 1/4 cup red wine vinegar
- 1 tbsp lemon juice
- 1 tbsp fresh oregano (or 1 tsp dried)
- 1 clove garlic, minced
- sea salt & black pepper to taste, freshly ground (about 1/4 tsp each)
- *If you'd like, use your favorite red wine vinaigrette or even Italian (I love Newman's Own) and add oregano.

Direction

- Whisk dressing ingredients together until well incorporated.
- Toss salad ingredients with dressing in a large bowl until well-distributed. Leftover dressing can be refrigerated in an air-tight container.

70. Mediterranean Pasta Salad Recipe

Serving: 8 | Prep: | Cook: 40mins | Ready in:

Ingredients

- Vinaigrette:
- 1/4 cup red wine vinegar
- 1 tbsp. lemon juice
- 2 cloves garlic, minced
- 2 tsp. dried oregano
- salt and freshly ground pepper to taste
- 2/3 cup extra-virgin olive oil
- Salad:
- 2 cups uncooked penne pasta (I use whole-wheat)
- 1 19 oz. can chick peas, drained or 1 cup channa dall (split chickpeas cooked in boiling water for 30 min. or until tender)
- 10 cherry tomatoes, cut in half
- 1 small red onion, coarsely chopped
- 1 yellow pepper, coarsely chopped
- 1 red pepper, coarsely chopped
- 1/2 english cucumber, sliced
- 1/2 cup pitted olives, sliced
- 1/2 cup feta cheese, crumbled

Direction

- To make the Vinaigrette:
- In a small bowl, whisk together the red wine vinegar, lemon juice, garlic, oregano, salt and pepper and olive oil until combined. Set aside until ready to use.
- To assemble the salad:
- Bring a pot of salted water to boil. Add the pasta and cook until just tender. Drain and rinse under cold running water until cooled.
- If you are using Chana Dal instead, put measured amount in water on saucepan on the stove and bring to a boil. Turn down the heat and cook until tender, approximately 1/2 hour.
- Place the pasta in a large bowl and add the chickpeas (or the Chana Dal), tomatoes, feta cheese, red onion, yellow and red peppers, cucumber and olives.
- Pour on the vinaigrette and toss the salad well. This can be done ahead of time and stored, covered with plastic wrap and refrigerated for a few hours.

71. Mediterranean Potato Salad Recipe

Serving: 6 | Prep: | Cook: 40mins | Ready in:

Ingredients

- 1 1/2 lbs. new potatoes, quartered
- 3/4 c. boiling vegetable or chicken broth (salt-free)
- 1/2 c. Sun dried tomatoes (not in oil)
- 1 T. extra virgin olive oil
- 1 T. wine vinegar (white or red)
- 1/2 t. dried basil
- 1/4 t. black pepper
- 1 clove garlic, minced
- 1/2 c. sliced scallions
- 1/2 c. diced celery

Direction

- Cook potatoes in boiling water in a large saucepan for about 10 minutes, or until tender.
- Meanwhile, place dried tomatoes in a small bowl and cover with hot broth and set aside.
- Place olive oil, vinegar, basil, pepper and garlic in a blender or food processor.
- When dried tomatoes are soft, add to blender along with soaking liquid.
- Blend or process on high speed until nearly smooth (small bits of tomato will remain).
- Drain potatoes and transfer to a serving bowl and toss with the green onion, celery, and dressing.
- Allow to stand 30 minutes.
- Stir before serving.

72. My Big Fat Greek Salad....with Souvlaki Esque Chicken Recipe

Serving: 4 | Prep: | Cook: 20mins | Ready in:

Ingredients

- 1 package raw chicken tenderloins
- 1 head of iceberg lettuce (I prefer romaine, but iceberg was all that i had)
- 1 12oz can black pitted olives (or Greek olives), halved
- 1 small onion
- 8-10 pepperoncini peppers
- 2 plum tomatoes
- 1/2 cucumber
- 3 cloves garlic
- olive oil
- Dried oregano
- salt and fresh cracked pepper
- red wine vinegar
- garlic powder
- onion powder
- thyme
- mayonnaise
- feta cheese
- pita bread (homemade pita chips) 1-2 per person
- Non-stick spray

Direction

- Place chicken tenderloins in a bowl with 2 minced garlic cloves, about 4 tbsp. olive oil, 1 tsp. salt, cracked pepper, 1 tbsp. thyme, 1 tbsp. oregano, and 1/4 cup red wine vinegar. Marinate for an hour, or longer.
- Bake chicken in oven at 350 for 30 min, until brown. I used a toaster oven, and the last 10 minutes I switched from bake to toast. Adds great color!!
- In the meantime, prepare salad. Shred lettuce, slice onions, add pepperoncini peppers and olives, and slice plum tomatoes and cucumbers. Top with feta cheese to your preference. Let chicken cool slightly, cut into bite-sized pieces and top salad.
- Dressing:
- In a small container combine 3-4 tbsp. olive oil and red wine vinegar. Season liberally with salt and pepper. Add garlic powder, onion powder, oregano, about 1 to 1 1/2 tsp. Add a

dollop of mayonnaise to thicken slightly. Add 1 tbsp. of feta cheese and mix to combine.
- Pita Chips:
- Cut pita bread into quarters and separate top from bottom. Place on a cookie sheet sprayed with non-stick spray. Season with salt, pepper, onion powder and 1 garlic clove, finely minced. Bake at 250 for 10 minutes, then increase temperature to 350 for an additional 10 minutes. Every 5-7 minutes remove pita chips and move them around to ensure even cooking. Ovens may vary, bake until crispy.

73. Orzo Salad Recipe

Serving: 8 | Prep: | Cook: 10mins | Ready in:

Ingredients

- 1 cup uncooked orzo
- 2 cups chopped fresh basil
- 1/2 cup chopped oil packed sundried tomatoes, drained
- 3 Tblsp chopped red onion
- 3 Tblsp chopped pitted kalamata olives
- 1/2 tsp freshly ground pepper
- 1/4 tsp salt
- 1 6 oz jar marinated artichoke hearts, undrained
- 3/4 cup feta cheese

Direction

- Cook orzo according to directions. Drain, rinse with cold water. Combine orzo & next 6 ingredients in a large bowl. Drain artichokes, reserving marinade. Coarsely chop artichokes & add them & reserved marinade to orzo mixture, tossing gently to coat. Sprinkle with feta cheese & toss again. Drizzle with olive oil if it is too dry.

74. Party Size Greek Couscous Salad Recipe

Serving: 12 | Prep: | Cook: 20mins | Ready in:

Ingredients

- 3 (6 ounce) packages garlic and herb couscous mix (or any flavor you prefer)
- 1 pint cherry tomatoes, cut in half
- 1 (5 ounce) jar pitted kalamata olives, halved
- 1 cup mixed bell peppers (green, red, yellow, orange), diced
- 1 cucumber, sliced and then halved
- 1/2 cup parsley, finely chopped
- 1 (8 ounce) package crumbled feta cheese
- 1/2 cup Greek vinaigrette salad dressing

Direction

- Cook couscous according to package directions.
- Transfer to a large serving bowl to cool.
- Stir to break up clusters of couscous.
- When the couscous has cooled to room temperature, mix in tomatoes, olives, bell peppers, cucumber, parsley, and feta.
- Gradually stir vinaigrette into couscous until you arrive at desired moistness.

75. Pita Panzanella Recipe

Serving: 4 | Prep: | Cook: 10mins | Ready in:

Ingredients

- five mini wheat toasted pita breads
- 1/2 of red pepper, diced
- 1 bunch of green onion, cleaned and sliced
- 1/2 cup of cherry tomatoes, halved
- 1/2 tsp of oregano
- 1/2 tsp of dried mint, crumbled in your fingers
- 2 tbsp of red wine vinegar
- 2 tbsp of olive oil

- 1/3 cup or more of crumbled feta

Direction

- Toast the bread slightly.
- Cool
- Quarter pitas
- Toss with veggies
- Dress with vinegar and oil
- Sprinkle with herbs
- Toss with feta
- Grind some fresh pepper over all
- Stir and let the dressing soak into the pita
- Serve it up and dig in.

76. Quick And Healthy Greek Potato Salad Recipe

Serving: 4 | Prep: | Cook: 20mins | Ready in:

Ingredients

- Ingredients:
- 1 ½ pounds russet potatoes (red, yellow or white potatoes can be substituted)
- 1 cup low-fat 2% Greek yogurt (such as Chobani, FAGE, Oikos or YoPlait)
- 1/3 cup minced red onion
- 1/4 cup sliced kalamata olives
- 1/4 cup peeled, chopped cucumber
- 1 tablespoon lemon juice
- 1/4 teaspoon sea salt
- Freshly ground pepper to taste
- Chopped fresh parsley
- 1/2 cup crumbled feta cheese
- Chopped fresh oregano (optional)

Direction

- Instructions:
- Place whole potatoes (do not poke) into microwave-safe dish. Cover dish. (If covering dish with plastic wrap, poke small hole in plastic).

- Microwave on high for 10 to 12 minutes depending on strength of microwave.
- Use oven mitts to remove dish from microwave; carefully remove cover from dish due to steam build-up and let cool.
- Cut potatoes into bite-size pieces and place in a large bowl with remaining ingredients; stir well to mix.
- Sprinkle with cheese and oregano.
- This salad may be served right away, but is best if refrigerated for at least one hour to allow flavors to blend.

77. Quick And Light Greek Salad Recipe

Serving: 6 | Prep: | Cook: | Ready in:

Ingredients

- 3 cucumbers halved seeds removed and sliced
- 3/4 cup crumbled feta cheese
- 1/2 cup sliced canned black olives drained
- 3 cups diced roma tomatoes
- 1/3 cup julienne sun dried tomatoes oil only lightly drained off
- 2/3 cup chopped red onion

Direction

- Add all ingredients to a salad bowl and gently toss.
- Cover bowl and chill in refrigerator until ready to serve.

78. Salad With Chick Peas Sausages Recipe

Serving: 4 | Prep: | Cook: 35mins | Ready in:

Ingredients

- 3 tbs red whine vinegar
- 2 tbs olive oil
- 2 cloves garlic pressed
- 1 lemon (zest and juice)
- 600 gr chick peas
- 125 gr sausages (I use piquant) peeled and cut in cubes
- 1 medium onion sliced
- 1 red bel pepper sliced
- 1 small cucumber seeded and cut in cubes
- 3 ts mint chopped
- 3 ts parsley chopped
- 3 ts coliander chopped
- salt to taste
- fresh black pepper to taste
- 3 ts celery leaves chopped

Direction

- Soak chick peas overnight in cold water, whoever wants can use from can. I prefer to cook them fresh.
- Wash cap under cold streaming water and drain.
- Cook cap 30 min in the pressure cooker, drain and let cool down.
- Stir/fry sausage cubes in a frying pan 3 min (dry) and let cool down
- Put vinegar, olive oil, lemon zest/juice, garlic in a big bowl and mix.
- Add chick peas, sausages, onion, bell pepper and cucumber.
- Add salt and pepper to taste and mix well.
- Mix aromatic herbs and top on salad, slightly mix and serve.

79. Seafood Salad Recipe

Serving: 4 | Prep: | Cook: 50mins | Ready in:

Ingredients

- 1 bunch arugula or rocket.
- 1 lettuce.
- 1 small radichio (red cabbage).

- 3 spring onions thinly sliced.
- 1 small leek thinly sliced.
- 10 cherry tomatoes cut in halves.
- 1/2 cup dill chopped.
- 1 medium yellow onion thinly sliced.
- 1/2 c parsley chopped.
- 1 celery stalk thinly sliced.
- 7 small squids.
- 30 mussels cleaned.
- 1 small octopus cleaned.
- 30 medium shrimps, shell and tale of.
- 1 c balsamic vinegar.
- For the dressing;
- 150 gr olive oil.
- 1 ts balsamic vinegar.
- juice of 1 1/2 lemon.
- 1 tbs mustard.
- 1 ts honey.
- salt and pepper to taste.

Direction

- Clean salads, drain, dry and tear in rough pieces.
- Put octopus in a pan, cover with vinegar, cook till softened (ca 20min), cool and cut in 5 cm pieces.
- In a frying pan sauté the mussels in their fluid ca 5 min, throw away those which don't open, take mussels out shells.
- Cook squids ca 20 min, add shrimps and cook 5 min more on low heat.
- Slice squids in 1/2 cm pieces.
- In a bowl mix all seafood.
- On a big salad plate mix salads, herbs, spring onion, leek, onion, celery, and cherry tomatoes, top with seafood.
- Beat dressing ingredients add salt and pepper to taste and sprinkle over salad.
- Serve with warm brown bread (baguette) and cold white whine

80. Shepherd's Salad Recipe

Serving: 6 | Prep: | Cook: 15mins | Ready in:

Ingredients

- 3 roma tomatoes,seeded and chopped
- 2 cucumbers,seeeded and chopped
- 1 bunch parsley,leaves picked,not chopped
- 1/2 c pitted and halved black olives
- 1/2 small red onion,chopped
- 2 TB cider vinegar
- 2 TB lemon juice
- 4 TB olive oil
- salt and fresh ground black pepper
- 8 oz Greek feta cheese,diced

Direction

- Toss together all ingredients except feta cheese in large bowl. Let sit at room temperature for 1 hour to allow flavors to develop. Toss in feta cheese just before serving and taste for seasoning and adjust, if necessary.

81. Summer Orzo Salad Recipe

Serving: 128 | Prep: | Cook: 8mins | Ready in:

Ingredients

- Ingredients:
- 4C chicken broth
- 4C water
- 1lb. orzo
- 1-3/4 C extra virgin olive oil, divided
- 4C baby spinach leaves
- 1 1/2 C thinly sliced sundried tomatoes
- Grilled & Sliced boneless chicken breasts (approx. 3 breasts)(I marinate the chicken in Greek Dressing overnight.
- 1/2 C sliced kalamata olives
- 1 bunch green onions, finely chopped
- 1/2 C fresh basil, finely sliced
- 1/2 C pinenuts, toasted

- 2 (4 oz.) containers of feta cheese, crumbled
- juice of 1 lemon
- salt & pepper to taste

Direction

- Bring Chicken broth and water to a boil.
- Add orzo, cook according to directions & drain.
- Mix warm orzo with 1/2 C olive oil. Set aside until cool. Toss with spinach, tomatoes, olives, onions, basil, nuts, and cheese. Add 1/4C remaining oil and lemon juice. If mixture is too dry, add remaining 1/4 C oil. Season with S &P. Toss to mix lightly, but well. If making ahead cover & refrigerate up to 2 hours in advance. Bring to room temp. before serving. Add chicken breast to make into a main dish.

82. Super Easy And Super Tasty Greek Rice Salad With Grilled Chicken Recipe

Serving: 68 | Prep: | Cook: |Ready in:

Ingredients

- 2 1/2 cups cooked brown rice
- 1 cup diced cucumber
- 1 cup diced grilled chicken
- 1 cup diced seeded fresh tomatoes
- 1/2 cup sliced black olives
- 1/4 cup chopped red onion
- 1 tbs. chopped fresh basil
- 1 1/2 tsp. chopped fresh oregano
- 1 garlic clove, minced
- 1/4 cup olive oil
- 1/4 cup lemon juice
- 2 tbs. red wine vinegar
- salt and pepper to taste

Direction

- In a medium bowl, combine rice, cucumber, chicken, tomatoes, olives, onion, basil, oregano, and garlic.
- In a small bowl, whisk together oil, lemon juice, and vinegar.
- Pour oil mixture over the salad; toss to coat.
- Season with salt and pepper to taste.
- Chill overnight to allow flavors to meld.

83. Tomato Halloumi Salad Recipe Recipe

Serving: 4 | Prep: | Cook: 15mins | Ready in:

Ingredients

- 1kg fresh tomatoes, thinly sliced
- 200g halloumi cheese, diced
- 50ml vegetable oil, for frying
- 4 pcs pita bread
- Olive oil and Mint Dressing
- 60ml olive oil
- 1 tbsp fresh mint, finely chopped
- salt and black pepper to taste

Direction

- Heat oil in a saucepan and fry halloumi until golden brown. Drain well on absorbent paper.
- Toast or grill pita bread until lightly browned.
- Layer sliced tomatoes on the bottom of a plate, top with halloumi cheese and drizzle with olive oil and mint dressing.
- Serve with warm pita bread.

84. Tuna Pepper Pasta Salad Recipe

Serving: 4 | Prep: | Cook: |Ready in:

Ingredients

- 2 tablespoons nonfat plain yogurt

- 2 tablespoons chopped fresh basil
- 2 tablespoons water
- 1 1/2 teaspoons lemon juice
- 1 garlic clove, minced
- Freshly ground pepper (to taste)
- 2/3 cup roasted red peppers, chopped and divided
- 1/2 cup finely chopped red onion
- 4 oz chunk light tuna in water, drained
- 4 oz broccoli florets, steamed until crisp-tender and shocked
- 6 ounces whole-wheat penne, cooked and drained

Direction

- Combine yogurt, basil, water, lemon juice, garlic, salt, pepper and the remaining 1/3 cup red peppers in a blender, puree until smooth.
- In a large bowl, toss together remaining peppers, onion, tuna, broccoli and pasta.
- Add the pepper sauce and toss well to blend. Chill before serving.

85. WW Greek Pasta Salad Recipe

Serving: 8 | Prep: | Cook: | Ready in:

Ingredients

- Salad:
- 12 ozs (375 g) bow-tie pasta
- 2 2/4 cups (675 ml) diced tomatoes
- 1 cup (250 ml) diced cucumbers
- 1 cup (250 ml) diced sweet green peppers
- 3/4 cup (175 ml) sliced red onions
- 3 1/2 ozs (90 g) crumbled feta cheese
- 1/3 cup (75 ml) sliced black olives
- 1/2 cup (125 ml) chopped fresh oregano (or 1 tbsp (15 ml) dried)
- Dressing:
- 1/4 cup (50 ml) olive oil
- 3 tbsp (45 ml) lemon juice
- 2 tbsp (25 ml) water
- 2 tbsp (25 ml) balsamic vinegar

- 2 tsp (10 ml) crushed garlic

Direction

- Cook pasta according to package instructions or until firm to the bite. Rinse in cold water. Drain and place in a serving bowl.
- Add tomatoes, cucumbers, green peppers, onions, feta cheese, olives and oregano.
- Make the dressing: In a small bowl, combine oil, lemon juice, water, vinegar and garlic until mixed. Pour over pasta and toss.

86. Warm Grecian Salad Recipe

Serving: 4 | Prep: | Cook: 35mins | Ready in:

Ingredients

- 6 medium red potatoes, unpeeled and chopped
- 3 cups whole white mushrooms
- 2 carrots, peeled and chopped
- 2 medium zucchini, chopped
- 1 red onion, sliced
- 2 red peppers, chopped
- 4 cloves garlic, minced
- 2 tsp olive oil
- 1 tbsp rosemary
- 1 tsp dried oregano
- 2 tbsp balsamic vinegar
- 1 tsp black pepper
- 2 tsp red pepper flakes
- 2 oz soft goat cheese (optional)

Direction

- Preheat oven to 425F.
- Mix vegetables, garlic, oil and herbs.
- Pour into a roasting pan. Bake 30 minutes, stirring halfway through.
- Switch heat to broiler and cook a further 5 minutes.
- Transfer all to a serving bowl.

- Mix vinegar, pepper and pepper flakes. Pour over vegetables and toss.
- Crumble cheese over the dish and serve warm.

87. Water Melon & Feta Salad Recipe

Serving: 0 | Prep: | Cook: 15mins | Ready in:

Ingredients

- 1/2 water melon try some sweet n seedless
- 200 gms of feta
- salt n pepper to taste
- 80ml of olive oil
- some basil leaves for garnish

Direction

- Wash n cut the melon into 1/2 then with a scooper or a spoon scoop out some lovely round balls of watermelon or u cut into chunks it totally depends on you.
- In a mixing bowl add olive oil salt n pepper n just mix it a kind of dressing pour it on the water melon n let chill for couple of hour
- Before serving just add crumble feta n garnish with basil leaves try not to use knife to the cut leaves just with pluck it with hands
- Ready to serve. Can be served in the watermelon shell.
- Enjoy:-P
- Ps: if u like my recipes please rate it!!!! Thank you

88. Watermelon Salad Recipe

Serving: 0 | Prep: | Cook: 20mins | Ready in:

Ingredients

- 3 cups watermelon in chunks
- 1 cup chopped cucumber (in chunks)

- 1/2 cup crumbled feta cheese
- 2 tbsp mint
- 2 tbsp balsamic vinaigrette dressing

Direction

- Put all ingredients together I also added the cherry tomatoes

Index

Conclusion

Thank you again for downloading this book!

I hope you enjoyed reading about my book!

If you enjoyed this book, please take the time to share your thoughts and post a review on Amazon. It'd be greatly appreciated!

Write me an honest review about the book – I truly value your opinion and thoughts and I will incorporate them into my next book, which is already underway.

Thank you!

If you have any questions, **feel free to contact at:** *author@crostinirecipes.com*

Terra Mincy

crostinirecipes.com

Made in the USA
Middletown, DE
07 October 2023